STARS AND GALAXIES

Rebecca Clay

Series Editor:
Arthur Upgren, Professor of Astronomy
Wesleyan University

Twenty-First Century Books

A Division of Henry Holt and Company
New York

Twenty-First Century Books
A division of Henry Holt and Company, Inc.
115 West 18th Street
New York, New York 10011

Henry Holt® and colophon are registered trademarks of Henry Holt and Company, Inc.
Publishers since 1866

©1997 by Blackbirch Graphics, Inc.
First Edition
5 4 3 2 1
Published in Canada by Fitzhenry & Whiteside Ltd.
195 Allstate Parkway, Markham, Ontario L3R 4T8

Printed in the United States of America on acid free paper ∞.

Created and produced in association with Blackbirch Graphics, Inc.

Photo Credits

Cover (background) and page 4: ©NASA; cover (inset): ©John Wells/Science Photo Library/Photo Researchers, Inc.; p. 6: ©Jerry Schad/Science Source/Photo Researchers, Inc.; p. 9: ©John Sanford & David Parker/Science Photo Library/Photo Researchers, Inc.; p. 11: ©Jerry Schad/Photo Researchers, Inc.; pp. 13, 47: ©John Sanford/Science Photo Library/Photo Researchers, Inc.; p. 14: ©Kim Gordon/Science Photo Library/Photo Researchers, Inc.; p. 17: ©Dr. Jean Lorre/Science Photo Library/Photo Researchers, Inc.; p. 20: ©Tony Ward, Tetbury/Science Photo Library/Photo Researchers, Inc.; p. 21: Dr. Rudolph Schild/Science Photo Library/Photo Researchers, Inc.; pp. 22, 52, 54: Royal Observatory, Edinburgh/Science Photo Library/Photo Researchers, Inc.; p. 24: ©J. Baum & N. Henbest/Science Photo Library/Photo Researchers, Inc.; p. 27: AP/Wide World Photos; p. 28: ©Julian Baum/Science Photo Library/Photo Researchers, Inc.; pp. 31, 40: ©John Chumack/Photo Researchers, Inc.; p. 37: ©Space Telescope Science Institute/NASA/Science Photo Library/Photo Researchers, Inc.; p. 38: ©Dr. Seth Shostak/Science Photo Library/Photo Researchers, Inc.; p. 42: ©Tony Hallas/Science Photo Library/Photo Researchers, Inc.; p. 46: North Wind Picture Archives; p. 48: ©David A. Hardy/Science Photo Library/Photo Researchers, Inc.; p. 56: ©Julian Baum/New Scientist/Science Photo Library/Photo Researchers, Inc.

Library of Congress Cataloging-in-Publication Data

Clay, Rebecca
    Stars and galaxies / Rebecca Clay.
       p.   cm. — (Secrets of space)
    Includes bibliographical references and index.
    Summary: Describes the characteristics and movement of stars, the constellations they form, the composition and shapes of different galaxies, and more.
    ISBN 0-8050-4476-0
    1. Astronomy—Juvenile literature. 2. Stars—Juvenile literature. 3. Galaxies—Juvenile literature. [1. Stars. 2. Galaxies.] I. Title. II. Series.
QB46.C676   1997
523.8—dc21
                                 96-37363
                                     CIP
                                     AC

TABLE OF CONTENTS

INTRODUCTION

Humans have always been fascinated by space, but it has been only since the 1950s that technology has allowed us to actually travel beyond our Earth's atmosphere to explore the universe. What riches of knowledge this space exploration has brought us! All of the planets except Pluto have been mapped extensively, if not completely. Among the planets, only Pluto has not been visited by a space probe, and that will likely change soon. Men have walked on the Moon, and many of the satellites of Jupiter, Saturn, Uranus, and even Neptune have been investigated in detail.

We have learned the precise composition of the Sun and the atmospheres of the planets. We know more about comets, meteors, and asteroids than ever before. And many scientists now think there may be other forms of life in our galaxy and beyond.

In the *Secrets of Space* series, we journey through the wondrous world of space: our solar system, our galaxy, and our universe. It is a world seemingly without end, a world of endless fascination.

—Arthur Upgren
Professor of Astronomy
Wesleyan University

Even though the Milky Way contains billions of stars, we on Earth can see only about several thousand of them with the naked eye.

CHAPTER 1

STARRY, STARRY NIGHT

Step outside on any clear night, and what do you see overhead? No matter where you are, you will be standing under a black sky dotted with tiny points of light—stars, of course. Have you ever tried to count them? You will lose track fast!

Without a telescope, the only stars that we can see from Earth belong to our galaxy, the Milky Way. Although it may look like there are millions, a total of about 6,000 stars can actually be seen with the naked eye from Earth. Of those, 3,000 can be seen by people living in the Northern Hemisphere, and 3,000 by people living in the Southern Hemisphere. Even though it is *possible* to see this number of stars in each hemisphere, interference from things such as haze, moonlight, and man-made light would actually make viewing every one of those stars impossible.

Home Sweet Home

Most stars make their homes in galaxies, where they are joined by billions of other stars drawn together by gravity, and they revolve around a common nucleus. Together, they travel through space for millions, or even billions, of years. Galaxies come in various shapes and sizes—some are huge with long curving arms, while others are small with no definite shape. The Milky Way contains hundreds of billions of stars and is only one of at least 50 billion galaxies in the universe. No one knows exactly how many stars there really are.

Though stars may look like they are fixed in place, each one is actually speeding through its galaxy. Because they are so distant, however, we cannot perceive their movement. Over periods of thousands of years, their positions, and the patterns they make with other stars, change dramatically. Even the constellations—groupings of stars that appear to us to have patterns—have shifted slightly since our distant ancestors first noticed them thousands of years ago.

Count Your Lucky Stars

Where can you find a sea monster, a unicorn, a bull, a centaur, and a flying fox in the same place? In the night sky, of course! That is where you can spot the 88 constellations visible from Earth. If you look carefully enough, you will find that the heavens are full of fantastic creature-like shapes.

Long ago, people thought that the stars were fixed in place, that the points of light did not move. Greek farmers relied on star patterns to tell them when to plant and harvest their crops, and to guide them when they traveled long distances. Some cultures thought the stars were actually little lamps suspended in the sky. Central Americans imagined stars to be the glowing ends of cigars their dead heroes were smoking in heaven.

The early Greeks mapped celestial patterns and called the shapes constellations. Over 3,000 years ago, Greek storytellers created fabulous stories and myths and believed they saw images of their heroes in the patterns of the stars. Today, great mythological figures like the courageous Hercules and the beautiful Andromeda live on in the stars, in the constellations that have been named for them. The Egyptians, Chaldeans, Babylonians,

Here, an artist's rendering of a scorpion shows the creature superimposed on a photograph of the constellation the Greeks called Scorpius. (The stars that make up the constellation have been enhanced by the artist.)

Chinese, and Native Americans also saw familiar objects in the sky and incorporated them into their mythology.

Of course, the stars and constellations do not sit still. In one night, the stars seem to rise in the east and set in the west. This made many ancient peoples believe that the sky moved around Earth. Today, we know Earth is rotating on its axis from west to east. About two dozen constellations are usually visible at any one time because as Earth turns, some stars appear to set. Those constellations do not actually disappear, however, but can be seen from another region on Earth.

The bright star Polaris, or the North Star, does not seem to move because it appears at the top of Earth's axis and marks the North Pole. Polaris, also called the Pole Star, is the brightest star in the constellation Ursa Minor, or the Little Bear. Ursa Minor is best known as the Little Dipper. (Most people find it easier to spot a little dipper than a little bear.)

The most familiar star pattern in the sky is probably the Big Dipper. It is not really a constellation but an asterism, an easily recognizable group of stars within a constellation. The Big Dipper is made of seven stars from the huge constellation Ursa Major, the Great Bear. The Dipper's bowl contains four stars, while the handle has three.

The Little Bear and the Great Bear sprang from Greek mythology. In one myth, Zeus changed a young man and his mother into bears—the mother became the Great Bear and her son the Little Bear. On another continent, something about these stars also reminded Native Americans of bears. Many tribes believed that the bowl of the Big Dipper looked like a bear being chased by three hunters, the three stars of the handle.

The Big Dipper is one of the most recognizable star patterns in the sky.

As it has for thousands of years, the Big Dipper can help you find your way north. First, trace a line between the two stars at the end of the bowl farthest from the handle. These stars are called the Pointers because they point the way to the North, or Pole Star. When you follow this imaginary line, you will run into the North Star in the Little Dipper. If you are facing this star, you are facing north.

The location of an observer on Earth determines what constellations are visible to him or her. At the equator, a person can see all of the constellations. As a person travels away from the equator, either north or south, the visible constellations become fewer in number. For example, the Southern Cross cannot be seen from most areas of the United States and the Big Dipper is not visible from Australia.

Dragons and Queens

Most constellations rise and set depending on the season or time of night. Six always circle the North Pole, however, and never set. These circumpolar constellations are Ursa Minor, Draco (the Dragon), Camelopardalis (the Giraffe), Cepheus (the King), Cassiopeia (the Queen), and most of Ursa Major.

Two of the most interesting of these constellations are those named for Cassiopeia and her husband, Cepheus. Cassiopeia was a mythological Ethiopian queen, and her constellation is located in the Milky Way. Depending on where you are located, she may look either like the queen herself or like her throne. Cepheus's constellation looks like a huge head with a triangular cap and a pigtail. The best time to spot the two monarchs is August through January.

One of the most admired of all the constellations is Orion the Hunter. He really looks like his name. A triangle of three stars marks his head, and another three stars in a straight line reveal his belt, from which dangles his sword. His two hands hold a shield and the mighty club he uses to fight his enemy, Taurus the Bull. Orion has more bright stars than any other constellation, including the stars Rigel and Betelgeuse. Because his stars are so bright, Orion can be easily seen from both the city (where bright lights sometimes interfere with stargazing) and the country. Beside Orion are his faithful hunting dog constellations, Canis Major and Canis Minor.

Taurus the Bull was an Egyptian god in the ancient world. Bulls were often worshipped by ancient cultures. Two star clusters mark Taurus: the Hyades, which makes up the bull's

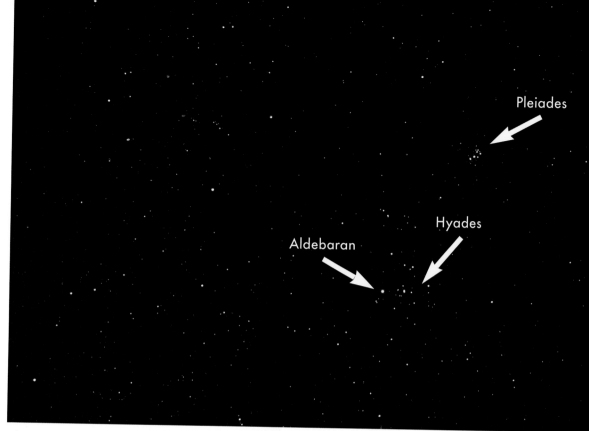

The constellation Taurus is marked by the star Aldebaran (below and just right of center), the Hyades star cluster (just to the right of Aldebaran), and the Pleiades star cluster (toward the upper right).

face, and the Pleiades, six small stars on his shoulder. The bull's eye is the great star Aldebaran. In ancient times, when Taurus appeared in the sky, people knew fall was on its way.

The constellation Leo the Lion dominates the spring sky. You can pick him out by the backward question mark that traces his head and shoulders. Leo is also home to the twenty-first brightest star, Regulus. The ancient Persians called Regulus "the Guardian of Heaven" and believed that it ruled the other stars.

Galaxies contain billions of stars and are found in various shapes. This photograph shows a spiral galaxy.

CHAPTER 2

ISLANDS IN THE SKY

While a constellation is a small group of stars that form a recognizable pattern, a galaxy contains billions of stars that have formed together in one region of the universe. The force of gravity holds the stars together as they orbit around the center of the galaxy. Gravity is one of the most important forces in the universe—it is the force of attraction that exists between two bodies. Gravity is what holds a star together and what crushes its core at the end of its life. It brings gas and dust together into a ball to form a star and causes the star to explode when the gas has been used up. Gravity also brings stars together into pairs, multiple star systems, and galaxies. Without gravity, the universe would not exist in its present form.

With the invention of human-made satellites and spaceships, the second half of the twentieth century has been one of the most exciting times in the history of astronomy. In just a few decades, many mysteries about the nature of stars and galaxies have been solved, helping us to better understand our position in the universe. There is still so much more that remains to be explored and learned about the heavens.

Since 1990, the Hubble Space Telescope has been transmitting photographs of previously unseen parts of the universe back to Earth. Recent observations in 1996 by the Hubble Space Telescope indicate that there are at least 40 to 50 billion galaxies racing through outer space, including our own. It was previously believed that there were no more than 4 or 5 billion galaxies.

It is fascinating to consider our human existence against the backdrop of such an enormous universe. Think about it in this way: You, as an individual, were born into a family. Your family lives in a state that is part of a country. Your country exists on a planet called Earth. Earth is one of the planets in a solar system that revolves around the Sun. The Sun is one of hundreds of billions of stars in our galaxy—the Milky Way.

You might think of a galaxy as a "star city" or an "island universe," separated from other galaxies by mostly empty space. The city has a central area, like a downtown, and outside areas, like suburbs. In addition to a galaxy's billions of stars, it also contains star clusters, nebulae, and probably millions of planets.

Galaxies come in a variety of sizes, from dwarf elliptical galaxies to supergiant ellipticals that contain thousands of billions of stars. Each galaxy is made of the same basic but distinctive parts: a flat galactic disk, halo, nucleus, nuclear bulge, arms, and corona. The disk contains clouds of gas and dust, the raw material used to create new stars. Surrounding the disk is a huge halo, in which the galaxy's oldest stars can be found. The halo and the nucleus, which both contain clouds of old stars, are thought to be the first galactic regions in which stars were born billions of years ago. Looking like a big blob near the center of a galaxy, the nuclear bulge is where billions of old stars swarm tightly together and frequently collide into each other. The younger stars are located in the galaxy's arms and tend to be born there. The corona is the outermost part of a galaxy and is still largely a mystery to astronomers. Scientists can only guess at its makeup, but they can detect its gravitational properties.

For decades, scientists have come up with different theories about the evolution of galaxies. Most scientists believe that galaxies began billions of years ago as gas clouds that collapsed

This computer enhanced photograph of the spiral galaxy M81 shows young stars (in blue) located in the galaxy's arms.

under their own gravity. As the clouds collapsed, they began to spin very fast, causing them to flatten into the disk-like shapes we see today. Another important theory is that groups of stars form a gigantic system that rotates around the dense center of the galaxy, the bulge.

Because no telescope was powerful enough to view a galaxy as it was forming, no one had been able to prove one theory or another. In 1996, however, scientists made an astounding discovery. That is when the Hubble Space Telescope sent back detailed photographs of 18 densely packed star groups that contained about a billion stars each. The images showed

What Is a Light-year?

Each star is at its own particular stage of evolution. A few of the stars we see today no longer exist! They have either exploded or fizzled out. What we are actually seeing is the light they emitted during their lifetimes—beams that continue to travel through space long after a star has died. Because space is so enormous, astronomers usually do not measure the distances between celestial objects in terms of miles or kilometers. Instead, they describe these distances in terms of light-years.

A light-year is the distance that a beam of light travels in a vacuum in one year—5,878 trillion miles (9,458 trillion kilometers). Light travels at about 186,000 miles (299,000 kilometers) per second. The star closest to Earth—besides the Sun—is Proxima Centauri, 4.3 light-years away. This means it would take light about four years and three months to travel from Proxima Centauri to Earth. Or, if a spaceship could travel at the speed of light, it would arrive at Proxima Centauri four years and three months after leaving Earth.

events that took place about 11 billion years ago. According to the images, these star groups were gradually drawn together by gravity. Scientists suspect that a billion years later, the stars collided and merged to become a galaxy. We are able to see them now because it took the light from the star groups 11 billion years to reach us!

Pinwheels in the Sky

Galaxies are known by their shapes—spiral, elliptical, and irregular. More than two thirds of the thousand brightest galaxies in the sky are spiral galaxies. There are two basic types of spiral galaxies: open spiral and barred spiral. Our Milky Way and the nearby Andromeda galaxy are the two largest spiral galaxies in our region of the universe. The Andromeda galaxy's arms are more tightly wound than those of the Milky Way.

An open spiral galaxy has arms that seem to wrap around its center, or nucleus. From a great distance, an open spiral looks like a pinwheel. Spirals range in size from about 20,000 light-years to more than 100,000 light-years in diameter.

Some spiral galaxies have bands of stars and dust running through their centers. This special type of spiral galaxy is called a barred spiral. The spiral arms start at the ends of these bars and can be either tightly or loosely wound around the nucleus.

The Andromeda galaxy is named after the constellation Andromeda in which it appears. Although more than 2 million light-years away from Earth, the Andromeda galaxy is one of the few galaxies visible from Earth without a telescope. This galaxy contains about 300 billion stars. But since it is so far

The Andromeda galaxy, shown here in a false-color photograph, is a spiral galaxy located near our Milky Way.

away, it looks like a soft little patch of light in the night sky. The Andromeda galaxy is still, however, the farthest object that can be seen from Earth with the naked eye!

An elliptical galaxy looks like a spiral galaxy without the arms. Elliptical galaxies can be round or oval. Most appear to be very small and dim, making them difficult to see. The stars in elliptical galaxies are mostly middle-aged and older, and they have almost no gas or dust left to make new stars. These galaxies look like balls of old stars.

The most common galaxy is the dwarf elliptical, which can be as small as 5,000 light-years in diameter. The Draco galaxy, found in the constellation Draco, is a dwarf, and the dimmest

This false-color image of an oval elliptical galaxy shows five smaller galaxies being pulled toward its nucleus.

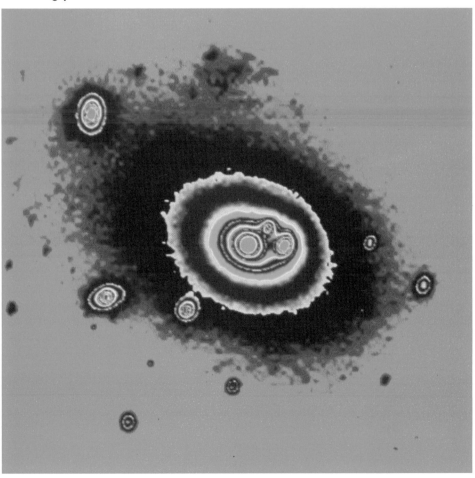

galaxy known so far. Even though it is a galaxy, Draco shines only four times more brightly than the star Rigel. Some giant ellipticals, on the other hand, may contain 10 to 100 times more stars than the Milky Way, and they are 10 times more luminous than the Andromeda galaxy.

Not every galaxy has a defined shape. Galaxies that are neither spiral nor elliptical appear irregular. Some may have gotten their odd shapes by colliding with other galaxies or from the gravitational pull of nearby galaxies. Irregular galaxies are usually smaller than other types, containing fewer than a thousand million stars.

The Large Magellanic Cloud is an irregular galaxy, which gets its name from its fuzzy appearance.

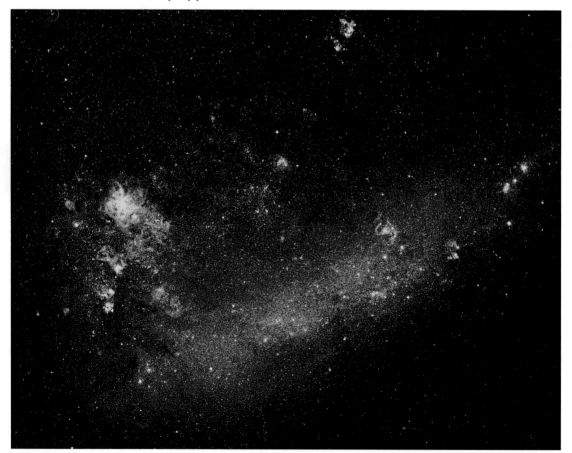

The Milky Way has two irregular galaxies as neighbors, or satellites, called the Large and Small Magellanic Clouds. These clouds can be seen easily from the Southern Hemisphere. They are called clouds rather than galaxies because they appear as fuzzy white patches in the sky. They are believed to be orbiting the Milky Way. The Magellanic Clouds got their name from the famous Portuguese explorer Ferdinand Magellan who saw them in 1519 during his voyage around the world. People living south of the equator, however, had seen these bright galaxies long before Magellan's first sighting because of their visibility to the naked eye.

At Home in the Milky Way

Set in the vast and sprawling universe, the Milky Way galaxy is our home. Since no spaceship has taken a telescope or camera outside the Milky Way, we have never actually viewed our own galaxy from beyond its borders. Our only view of it is the river of stars that runs across the sky on certain clear nights. Astronomers, however, have been able to determine the shape of the Milky Way by comparing it to neighboring galaxies. Some scientists disagree about whether the Milky Way is a barred or an open spiral galaxy.

The Milky Way is believed to be nearly a million trillion miles, or about 100,000 light-years, in diameter. A sprawling, spinning disk, the Milky Way may be only 10,000 light-years thick. It looks like two fried eggs, back to back, on their sides— a disc with a bulge in the middle. Seen straight on, like all spiral galaxies, it looks like a giant pinwheel.

This fabricated profile of the Milky Way shows a bulge in the middle of a thin disc.

Our Sun shares the Milky Way with more than 200 billion other stars, which all constantly revolve around the galaxy's giant nucleus. Each star travels at its own rate. Astronomers used to believe our solar system was at the center of the galaxy. Today, we know that our solar system is located about 30,000 light-years from the center. Traveling at a speed of about 130 miles (210 kilometers) per second, it takes the Sun 200 million years to revolve once around the galaxy. This long period of time is called a galactic year.

Astronomers have given each of the Milky Way's arms a name, such as the Orion Arm, the Perseus Arm, and the Sagittarius Arm. They still are not sure where the galaxy's boundaries lie. Many highly luminous supergiant stars are found along the arms, surrounded by bright, glowing clouds of charged hydrogen. Supergiants are young, as stars go—about 10 million years old— so scientists believe that the galaxy's arms may provide the right conditions for the birth of new stars.

The Backbone of Night

Ancient peoples were mystified by the streak of cloudy white that appeared in the clear night sky. To explain the existence of the Milky Way, they developed myths, which were handed down from generation to generation.

In Greek mythology, Hera, who was the wife of Zeus and goddess of the heavens, was tremendously powerful. The Greek people believed that the Milky Way was milk from Hera's breasts, which spilled across the heavens. *Gala* is the Greek word for milk. The Romans later changed the name to the *Via Lactea*, or Milky Way.

The !Kung Bushmen of Botswana in Africa believed that the Milky Way was a great barrier, which protected humans from being devoured by the monstrous beasts of darkness who lived on the other side. They called the Milky Way "the backbone of night," because that is when they thought the beasts hunted for victims on Earth.

Some Aborigines in Australia believed that the Milky Way was smoke from a campfire, which the Creator built after an exhausting time creating the stars and galaxies. Some Native Americans thought it was the road that brave warriors followed to heaven after they died.

The Chinese created a romantic story to describe the Milky Way, which they believed was a heavenly river. Two bright stars shine on each side of this river—Vega and Altair. In this Chinese myth, Vega was the daughter of the Sun god and a weaver of very beautiful fabrics. Altair was a herdsman who took care of the Sun god's cattle. Vega and Altair met and fell in love. They began spending so much time together that Vega stopped weaving and Altair forgot to tend the cattle. When the Sun god found out about the lovers he became furious. He decided to separate them, placing them far apart, on opposite sides of the river. But the brokenhearted Vega made her father promise that once a year he would allow a bridge of birds to cross the Milky Way's water and briefly reunite the two lonely lovers.

Bright Light from a Tiny Lightbulb

A quasar is one of the oldest and most mysterious objects in the universe. The name comes from quasi-stellar radio source because quasars send out strong radio waves. A quasar looks like an extremely bright blue star. Using the 200-inch (508-centimeter) Palomar telescope in California in the early 1960s, astronomer Allan Rex Sandage produced the first images of quasars, but he was unable to identify what they were. In 1963, astronomers Maarten Schmidt and Jesse Greenstein also observed these strange objects, bright enough to be collections of billions of stars, but far too small to be galaxies. The astronomers were amazed; here was the first evidence of a very distant and tiny object that burned as brightly as a galaxy. It was a major new discovery—a quasar.

Thousands of quasars have already been identified. They are so far away that they are believed to be among the first objects to come into existence. The most remote are over 15 billion light-years away. Although quasars were once common throughout the universe, there are relatively few of them today. They are thought to eventually evolve into galaxies. The Milky Way may once have been a quasar.

Quasars travel very fast, nearly the speed of light. They generate enormous

Like other galaxies, the Milky Way belongs to a cluster of galaxies called the Local Group. It includes over 26 member galaxies spread over a region about 3 million light-years in diameter. The Milky Way and Andromeda galaxy are the largest galaxies in the Local Group. Compared to other clusters, the Local Group is relatively small. In contrast, the Virgo Cluster has almost 2,000 member galaxies. Astronomers have spotted amounts of energy. Some are 60,000 times as bright as the entire Milky Way and produce more energy than 2,000 ordinary galaxies. Strangely enough, most quasars are believed to be much smaller than ordinary galaxies, perhaps only one light-year across—100,000 times smaller than the Milky Way!

What's going on? How does something so small produce so much energy and light? Astronomers disagree on the answers to these important questions. Some suggest that quasars are closer to Earth than commonly believed. Some think that they are the extremely bright centers of very young, developing galaxies. Others wonder if quasars are themselves galaxies, each with a giant black hole at

Maarten Schmidt

the center. Still others believe quasars are actually two separate galaxies that collided with each other, back when the universe was younger and more crowded.

several galaxy clusters less than 250 million light-years away, close enough to distinguish features of individual members.

Like some stars, galaxies occasionally consume their neighbors. The gravity from a larger and more powerful galaxy will draw a weaker galaxy toward it, eventually sucking it in and enveloping it. For example, the Milky Way is slowly devouring the Sagittarius spherical dwarf galaxy and all of its stars.

This artist's illustration depicts two young, bright stars in a cloud of stellar gas.

CHAPTER 3

THOSE STARTLING STARS

Stars glow because they are enormous and extremely hot.
During their lifetimes, stars create light and heat by burning
the gases they are made of—mostly hydrogen and helium.
These fuels generate enough energy to keep stars shining for
millions of years. We observe this energy in the form of starlight. When a star runs out of fuel, however, it begins to die
and to lose its light and heat.

When scientists study a star, they carefully examine its unique
characteristics. These include brightness (luminosity), size, mass,
age, color, and what chemicals it is made of. With this information, each star is then classified. A quick look at the night

sky will make you think all the stars are white. But take a closer look with a telescope and you will discover that stars come in a wide range of colors, including blue and red. By its individual color, scientists can tell a star's size, temperature, age, and chemical makeup.

A star's color is determined by its temperature. The cooler a star is, the redder it is. Usually, a red star is also an older star. Betelgeuse, in the constellation Orion, is a deep red color. Called a red supergiant, Betelgeuse is about 450 million miles (724 million kilometers) in diameter. The hottest stars are white and blue. These hot stars are usually very young. Rigel, also in Orion, is blue. Rigel is one of the brightest stars in the sky and burns about 50,000 times brighter than the Sun. In between, middle-aged stars glow in shades of orange and yellow.

Scientists use a spectroscope to separate starlight into its component colors and create a stellar spectrum. The spectroscope was invented in 1859 by German scientists Gustav Robert Kirchhoff and Robert Wilhelm Bunsen. This simple instrument works by letting a beam of light enter it through a tiny slit. The beam passes through a prism and is divided into its component colors. A stellar spectrum is thus created.

Stars are then classified into seven types, or spectral classes, according to temperature—O, B, A, F, G, K, and M. An O-type star is the hottest while an M-type is coolest. These letters also describe the stars' colors. For example, the O-type is blue, G-type stars like our Sun are white to yellow, and M-type stars glow a deep reddish color.

The brightest stars are usually the hottest and may shine a million times more brightly than the Sun. They are called

Betelgeuse is a red supergiant in the constellation Orion the Hunter.

supergiants. The smallest are cool and faint, often 1,000 times dimmer than supergiants. In general, star surface temperatures usually range from 3,000° F (1,650° C) to more than 60,000° F (33,782° C). Their interior temperatures burn much hotter.

The hottest stars can form planetary nebulae—the cores of stars that have partially blown up. Their surface temperatures can reach highs of 180,000° F (99,882° C). The coolest and dimmest stars are red dwarfs, which glow faintly at less than 4,500° F (2,480° C).

The Sun is our most important star. Without its light and heat, life as we know it on Earth would not exist. Located about 93 million miles (150 million kilometers) from our planet, the Sun is a medium-sized yellow star in the middle of its life. Its surface temperature is about 10,000° F (5,532° C), while the core burns at about 27 million° F (15 million° C). If the Sun were viewed from outside our solar system, it would look just like any other star its size.

Giant and supergiant stars are hundreds of times larger than our Sun, while *some* dwarf stars are hundreds of times smaller. (Compared to other stars, the Sun is medium-sized, an average star. Because it is yellow and relatively small, however, astronomers define it as a yellow dwarf star.) Some dwarf stars are only 1,000 miles (1,600 kilometers) across. Neutron stars are even smaller, sometimes no larger than 12 miles (20 kilometers) across; a car could drive from one end to the other in 20 minutes at average highway speed. Although they may be tiny by star standards, neutron stars are by far the most dense. A tablespoon of neutron star matter could weigh a billion tons—equal to about a billion small cars!

The spiral arms of the Milky Way galaxy are home to many highly luminous blue-white supergiants, many of which are surrounded by bright, glowing clouds of charged hydrogen. These hydrogen clouds can be seen by scientists using optical telescopes and can be detected with radio telescopes. Blue supergiants are the heaviest normal stars, as much as 50 or 60 times heavier than the Sun. Supergiants are also young stars—they are only about 10 million years old.

Any More Suns Out There?

One way scientists measure astronomical distances is by studying shifts in the color of a star's light waves as the star speeds through space. This shift is called the Doppler effect, named after Austrian physicist Christian Doppler, who discovered it in 1842. The Doppler effect is used for measuring both sound and light waves. It is sometimes easier to understand when referring to sound rather than light. For example, if a train is moving toward you, its whistle becomes louder, and as it moves away, the sound becomes lower and gradually disappears. The idea is similar with light waves. When viewed from Earth, each star exhibits the lines of a color spectrum. If the lines shift toward the violet on the color spectrum, the star is moving toward Earth. If the shift is toward the red, the star is moving away. The Doppler effect allows scientists to study and calculate how Earth and a star are moving in relation to each other.

Some scientists suspected that, like the Sun, other stars were also orbited by planets, creating other solar systems like our own. Astronomers used the Doppler effect to look for such planets.

One of the most exciting areas of astronomy today is the search for as yet unknown planets. One telltale sign of a planet in space is a slight wobble in a star's path as a planet's gravity pulls on it, creating subtle shifts in the starlight. Since the fall of 1995, at least eight stars have revealed such wobbles, suggesting that they are being tugged on by orbiting planets.

Scientists hope one day to find life on planets in other solar systems, or in other galaxies. Such planets are difficult to see because the glare from starlight hides them as they orbit. In

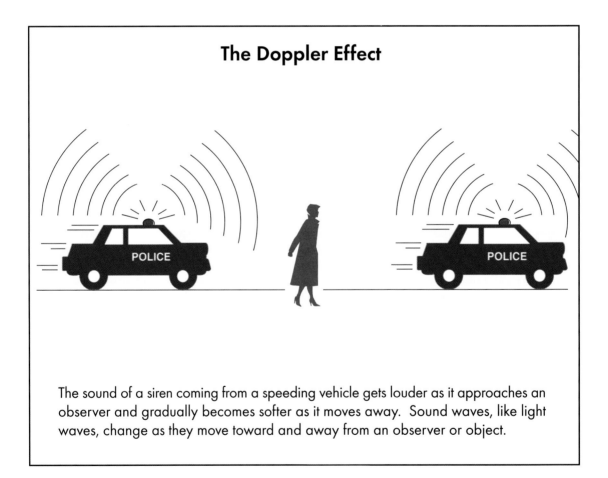

The Doppler Effect

The sound of a siren coming from a speeding vehicle gets louder as it approaches an observer and gradually becomes softer as it moves away. Sound waves, like light waves, change as they move toward and away from an observer or object.

the search for previously undiscovered planets, scientists are most interested in those that have temperatures neither too hot nor too cold to support life. It is believed that as many as half of the Milky Way galaxy's 200 billion stars may be orbited by planets. Scientists have observed such nearby stars as Alpha Centauri A and B, Epsilon Eridani, and Tau Ceti, to see if they have the characteristics (as the Sun does) needed to support life on nearby planets.

Epsilon Eridani is a yellow dwarf star about 11 light-years from Earth. It is less than 1 billion years old, however, which is too young by star standards to be able to provide a possible environment for intelligent life on any planets nearby. (Keep in mind that it took 4 billion years for higher life-forms to evolve on Earth.) Tau Ceti, a yellow star also located 11 light-years away from our planet, is a possibility because it may be the right age. Tau Ceti, however, may not contain the right metallic ingredients to support a planet like Earth where life might develop. At this point in time, astronomers are most interested in Alpha Centauri A and B because they most closely resemble the Sun: stable, rich in the right kind of metals, and about the same age.

Scientists have also noticed several regions outside the Milky Way galaxy with very young stars surrounded by disks of gas and dust that could be the beginnings of brand new solar systems. When the Sun was young, it was probably also surrounded by a belt of gas and dust. When gas and dust are brought together by gravity, the right conditions exist for new stars and planets to be created. It probably took a few hundred million years for the planets in our solar system to fully develop.

Spying on the Universe

Have you ever taken a telescope out to your backyard or to a nearby hilltop to view the stars? If you have, you would be using just one of many telescopes that are spying on the universe today. Each one is searching for new clues to unlock the secrets of the cosmos, including unknown objects and signs of extraterrestrial life.

Around the world, hundreds of high-tech telescopes are keeping an eye on the night sky around the clock. Most telescopes are either optical or radio telescopes. An optical telescope relies on human vision to view objects. A radio telescope uses antennae to pick up radio waves that are then converted into images.

Most telescopes are located in remote areas where city lights and radio stations will not interfere with the reception of images. Another obstacle for all earth-bound telescopes is Earth's atmosphere. Moisture in the air can blur an image that is viewed through a telescope. That is why most important research telescopes are built in dry regions like deserts.

The largest optical telescopes in the world are the Keck telescopes at Mauna Kea Observatory in Hawaii. Keck I and Keck II both have mirrors measuring 387 inches (983 centimeters) in diameter. The Kecks are also referred to as reflecting, or reflector, telescopes because they use mirrors to help focus images.

The Keck II telescope is particularly unusual because the surface of its mirror is made up of 36 individual sections instead of one big section. Having different sections provides important advantages. For one thing, it makes Keck II lighter than other telescopes. In addition, the giant mirror is much easier to polish. Keeping a telescope's mirror perfectly clean is a very important job since a speck of dust might be mistaken for a strange celestial object.

Another kind of telescope is the radio telescope, which uses radio waves to

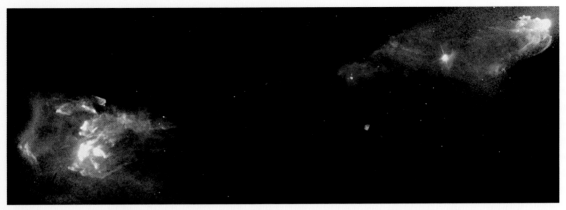

This image taken by the Hubble Space Telescope shows jets of gas being released from a young star.

create images of distant celestial objects. The largest is the Very Large Array (VLA) radio telescope located in New Mexico. The VLA uses 27 antenna dishes arranged along arms shaped like a Y. The VLA is able to produce very sharp images by combining the signals from each of the 27 dishes into one signal.

The most famous and exciting telescope in use now is the Hubble Space Telescope, which was launched in 1990. Today, the Hubble is sending back images and photographs of outer space that are astonishing the world. Hubble got off to a bad start. Its mirror was flawed; then different pieces of equipment began to break down. In 1993, however, a repair mission was sent up on the space shuttle *Endeavor* to fix the telescope's various problems. One of the great advantages to using the Hubble, rather than telescopes on the ground, is that it is positioned far above Earth's atmosphere. In this location, things like city lights and moisture in the air cannot prevent the telescope from producing clear images.

Colorful clouds of dust and gas are the nurseries of new stars, as seen in this artist's illustration.

CHAPTER 4

GREAT BALLS
OF FIRE!

One of the most awesome sights in the universe is a nebula, a vast and ever-shifting cloud of colorful gas and dust between the stars. Some nebulae are stellar nurseries—the places where stars are born.

A nebula is formed when a star blows up and dies. In the explosion, the star spews out the gas and dust that it was made of. Gravity continues to hold the star's shattered remains together as an interstellar cloud. Most of the gas in a nebula contains hydrogen atoms, along with helium, oxygen, and nitrogen.

Hydrogen makes up over three quarters of the matter in most stars and is the main fuel that keeps a star alive. The dust is made of particles, such as iron, carbon, calcium, sodium, magnesium, and titanium. When combined, these are most of the ingredients needed to make a brand new star.

A nebula does not send out its own light. It can only be seen when nearby stars shine on its gas and dust particles. One of the best known nebulae is the Great Orion Nebula. It is located in the constellation Orion the Hunter, 1,500 light-years from Earth, and stretches a few hundred light-years, or 20 billion miles (32 billion kilometers) across. The Great Orion Nebula has been incubating new stars for thousands of years.

The cloud of the Great Orion Nebula is illuminated by nearby stars.

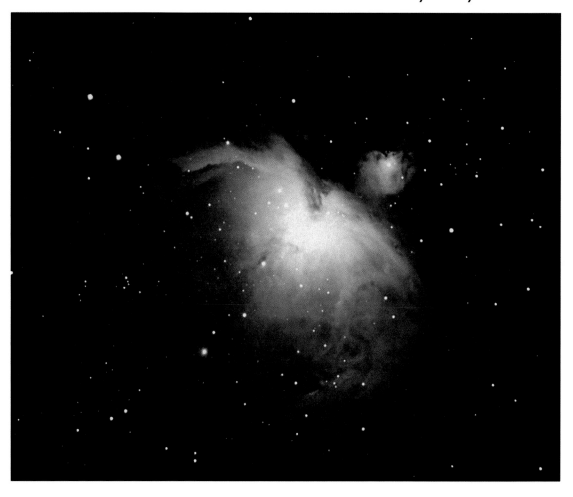

In late 1993, the Hubble Space Telescope discovered 15 young stars growing in the Great Orion Nebula's densest regions, behind the sword of the constellation Orion. What made the find most exciting for astronomers was the simultaneous discovery that flattened disks of dust and gas are spinning around each of these young stars. Scientists believe these "protoplanetary disks" could be the birthplace of new planets, moons, and solar systems like our own.

The Crab Nebula is the corpse of a supermassive star that blew apart in A.D. 1054, less than 1,000 years ago. The explosion was so intense that people all over the world saw its brilliant light both day and night. Native Americans were amazed that a fire could burn in the sunlit sky and Chinese astronomers wrote down every detail as the explosion continued to blaze overhead for several weeks. Today, we can still see the Crab Nebula at night because its original star continues to burn brightly, even though it has shrunk to just 10 miles (16 kilometers) in diameter—a ghost of its former self.

A Star Is Born

Stars are not born one at a time. Hundreds or thousands start forming around the same time from inside the same giant nebula. They also do not grow at the same rate. Learning about how stars evolve during their lifetimes is a field of scientific study called stellar evolution. Some stars take just millions of years to "grow up," while others develop slowly over billions of years. In the process, all of these stars share a common area within the nebula, forming an open cluster.

The Pleiades open cluster, seen in this optically enhanced image, contains stars that appear to be covered by a light cloud.

One of the best known open clusters is the Pleiades, in the constellation Taurus the Bull. The Pleiades is easy to spot with the naked eye in the night sky—it looks like a group of six tiny points of light floating close together. Using a telescope, it can be seen that the Pleiades actually contains hundreds of hot, bright stars surrounded by the gas and dust left over from their birth. Open clusters located in a galaxy are called galactic clusters. Several millions of years after new stars are born, open clusters start to break up and the stars drift apart.

No one knows exactly what triggers the formation of stars, but at some point gravity starts the process by drawing gas molecules and dust together into a ball called a globule. Over time, the globule starts to grow. The larger and denser it becomes, the more gas and dust its gravity pulls in.

As it starts to expand, the ball becomes a protostar, an immature version of a star. It continues to attract gas and dust onto its surface, but still has a long way to go before becoming a mature star. Millions of years later, the protostar becomes so big and heavy that it starts to suck its outer layers in toward its own core. The protostar is now collapsing into itself, putting extreme pressure on the core. The interior responds to this pressure by becoming extremely hot.

When the core of the protostar reaches several million degrees in temperature, the critical process of creating energy by nuclear fusion begins. Nuclear fusion turns lighter substances—mainly hydrogen—into (slightly) heavier substances—mainly helium—at extremely high temperatures. Nuclear fusion generates so much energy that the protostar's core can stop the outer layers from collapsing into it.

How to Make a Star

You'll need fewer ingredients to make a star than to make a batch of cookies, but it will take millions of years longer. If you have time, try this recipe. Warning: it cannot be done in an afternoon.

First, bring together a cloud of gas and dust. The gas should have mostly hydrogen in it, plus some helium, oxygen, and nitrogen. The dust should be made of tiny particles such as iron and sodium. You can call this cloud a nebula.

Pack some of the gas and dust together like a snowball, forming a globule. Keep adding gas and dust until the globule starts gaining weight. Now call this globule a protostar. Watch out, because when it gets too heavy, the protostar will start collapsing into itself. The outer layers will start pressing against the core. Be careful, this intense pressure will make the core heat up like a broiling oven!

Inside the core, nuclear fusion is taking place—hydrogen is converting itself to helium. With all that heat, the core will start expanding and pushing against the collapsing surface of the protostar. Both sides will be pressing so hard against each other that after a while they won't be able to budge, like a reverse tug-of-war.

You will know your ball is ready when it has turned into a flaming sphere—a shining star. Reach up on a clear night and place your great ball of fire into the inky black sky. (P.S. Don't really try this at home!)

When the star stops collapsing and its core stops pushing outward, the star can begin to stabilize. This allows it to burn its hydrogen and produce the powerful energy that creates starlight. After millions of years of gestation, a brand new star is finally born.

The time it takes for a globule to become a star depends on how massive it was in the beginning. Globules that start out large grow up and die much faster than smaller ones because their higher gravity attracts gas and dust more quickly. They also become so heavy that their outer layers collapse sooner and their cores heat up faster. That makes them use up their hydrogen sooner. A star begins to die when it consumes most of its hydrogen. Large stars begin to die after just a few million years. Our Sun is a medium-sized star and should live for billions of years. A small star can keep on shining for over 10 billion years.

Star Attractions

Because of their own gravity, and the gravity of their neighbors, stars are naturally attracted to one another. What looks like one star in the sky may actually be two stars circling each other. This is called a binary star. Binary stars can only be identified through an optical telescope or a spectroscope. British astronomer Sir William Herschel was the first to recognize binary stars in 1803.

Binary stars are common in the universe and come paired up in different ways. Most of the time, one of the binary stars is larger and brighter than the other. For example, a supergiant may be paired with a white dwarf. Their light appears brighter or dimmer as they revolve around each other. This occurs because one star will pass in front of the other, blocking or eclipsing the second star's light. The two stars look brightest when they are viewed side by side. Sirius, the brightest star in the night sky as seen from Earth, is actually a binary star, made up of Sirius A and Sirius B. It appears so bright because it is closer to Earth than almost all other stars—just 8.7 light-years away.

Sometimes the two stars get too close to each other. In what is called a contact binary star, the star with the most gravity slowly sucks out the gas and dust of the other. As the matter streams across the space between them, it becomes a whirlpool of hot gas, mostly hydrogen. The whirlpool keeps getting hotter and brighter until it suddenly blows up like a huge bomb. Ancient astronomers called this new kind of star a nova, because they believed the explosion signaled the birth of a new star. Novae can become as much as 200,000 times as bright as the original contact binary star before growing dimmer. At least a few novae are observed in the Milky Way each year.

When more than two stars are circling each other, they form a multiple star. Our closest multiple star, Alpha Centauri, is actually a triple-star system. The three stars

Sir William Herschel discovered binary stars in the early 1800s.

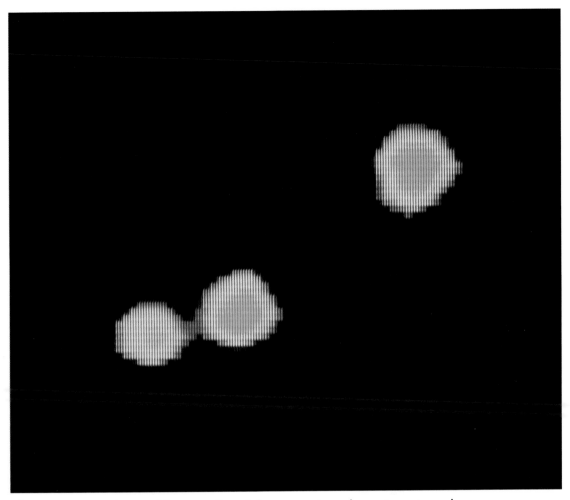

This computer-enhanced image of a triple-star system shows two stars close to each other, with a third nearby.

in this system orbit each other every 80 years. Of the three, Proxima Centauri is the smallest and closest to Earth. Its bigger and brighter siblings are Alpha Centauri A and B. Proxima Centauri is a red dwarf, 4.3 light-years away. A red dwarf is a small, light-weight star that is cool and faint. Red dwarfs are the most common type of star in space.

At the end of their lives, some stars die in a tremendous explosion called a supernova. Here, an artist's depiction shows a supernova and the shock waves that result from it.

CHAPTER 5

FROM STARDUST TO STARDUST

Although they keep shining for billions of years, we know that stars do not live forever. At some point, they begin to die, using up all their fuel and either fading out or blowing up. In the same way that it took millions or billions of years for a star to be born, it may take just as long to expire. A star begins the death process when its entire hydrogen supply is gone.

Each star dies in its own way and at its own pace. Small stars live longer than large ones because they burn their hydrogen more slowly and efficiently. The bigger a star is, the more hydrogen it needs to use to keep shining, and the faster it runs out of fuel. Compare it to a small car that can travel many more miles on one tank of gas than can a big car.

During its lifetime, a star burns its hydrogen by converting it to helium and creating heat and light. Once all the hydrogen is gone, the star can no longer create enough energy to prevent its outer layers from collapsing into its core. This inward pressure causes the core to heat up and swell. The star becomes unstable, sometimes expanding to become thousands of times brighter and bigger than it had been.

Eventually, the star stops expanding. With its much larger surface, the heat emitted by the star is spread out and the temperature drops. As the surface starts to cool, it begins to turn red. The star is now a red giant. If it were originally a very large star, it will turn into a red supergiant. All stars go through this red giant or red supergiant phase. Scientists believe that in about 5 billion years, our Sun will also turn into a red giant, growing so huge that it will swallow up its planets—including Earth.

The star's cool surface, however, is deceptive. Inside, its core is continuing to contract and heat up. Internal temperatures become so hot that the star begins to burn off its helium. In the process, the star is again using nuclear fusion to create heat and light, this time to convert its helium into carbon, a common substance on Earth. After millions of years, the star will use up all its helium and die.

Before its last gasp, however, the star struggles to stabilize itself and survive. It cools off and heats up, swells and contracts, appearing bright and then faint, again and again. Like a light connected to a dimmer switch, its brightness constantly changes. At this stage, scientists call it a variable star.

Eventually, the star loses control, and its outer shell begins to break up under the pressure. Its gaseous contents float out into

A Star's Telltale Heart

In 1784, astronomer John Goodriche was the first to notice two stars that seemed to pulsate— their light became first brighter and then dimmer on a regular and precise basis. These changeable stars were named Cepheids (pronounced see-fee-ids), after the most famous of them all, Delta Cephei.

Cepheids are yellow supergiants that pulsate like a human heart. The periods between pulsations can range from hours to hundreds of days. The longer the period, the brighter the star. This relationship between the length of the period and a star's brightness was discovered in 1912 by astronomer Henrietta Swan Leavitt of the Harvard College Observatory.

When Cepheids were discovered, many people became upset, especially those who had believed that the universe was perfect and changeless. The existence of a changeable star was frightening and disturbing. For many, it meant that the heavens were less stable and constant than everyone had previously thought. As a Cepheid expands and contracts, it brightens and dims, and its pulsations can be detected on Earth.

Eta Aquilae, the first Cepheid discovered, pulsates exactly once every 7.176779 days and never skips a beat. It is located in the summer constellation Aquila in the Milky Way galaxy. Cepheids are also found in other galaxies. Using the Cepheids' pulsations, astronomers can calculate the distance of these stars and their galaxies from the Milky Way.

the universe but stay together in the shape of a gigantic smoke ring. The star's core, however, continues to exist within the ring, and its fading light can make the ring glow for thousands of years. This huge, shining circle of gas is called a planetary nebula, and it is one of the most beautiful sights in the universe.

This ring of gas—a planetary nebula—surrounds the core of a dying star.

The planetary nebula got its name because it originally looked like a planet through a telescope. Scientists believe the Sun will probably pass through the planetary nebula stage when it dies.

Inside this nebula, gravity causes the star's core to continue collapsing into itself until it is as compact and dense as possible. It is now extremely small, heavy, and hot and is called a white dwarf. Most stars end their existence this way. Because all of its hydrogen and helium are gone, the white dwarf cannot make any more energy. Its core is now primarily made of carbon. A thimbleful of white dwarf matter would weigh about 10 tons. Sirius B is an example of a white dwarf.

A white dwarf eventually cools off and becomes a black dwarf—a burned-out chunk of very dense matter, like a lifeless cinder. Astronomers do not know whether or not there are any black dwarfs in the Milky Way.

A Dramatic Exit

Many of the biggest stars go out with a bang rather than a whimper, blowing up in brilliant explosions instead of just running out of gas. Their size makes big stars extremely heavy and their gravity squeezes their cores with great intensity. This inward pressure heats the core to such high temperatures that the star begins to convert its helium into iron, a common metal that marks the end of a large star's life.

Iron cannot create new energy to help the star stop the collapse of its core. Instead, the pull of the core's gravity causes it to suddenly collapse and explode. The star blasts its outer layers to smithereens, shooting out enormous amounts of gas at speeds of up to 10,000 miles (18,000 kilometers) per second. For a few weeks, this exploding heavyweight star shines as brightly as a billion ordinary stars. It's a supernova!

The most recent supernova in the Milky Way appeared in 1604, but astronomers observed one in a nearby galaxy in 1987.

The supernova of 1987, seen here on the lower right in this enhanced image, captured the attention of astronomers around the world.

The great clouds of gas and dust left behind by supernovae become nebulae, which contain the ingredients necessary for the formation of new stars. The Crab Nebula was formed from a supernova explosion.

Although a supernova itself is a cloud of debris, sometimes its dead core remains an extremely dense, mostly iron ball. Gravity has squeezed the core so hard it has collapsed into a neutron star, often just 12 miles (20 kilometers) across. A neutron star's matter is so tightly packed that scientists believe a piece of it the size of a marble would weigh billions of tons. If that marble were dropped from just a few feet above Earth's surface, it would instantly shoot through the entire 8,000-mile (12,900-kilometer) diameter of our planet. It would then race on into the universe on the other side of Earth at a speed of thousands of miles per second.

Sometimes neutron stars can be seen as one of the two stars in a binary star system. In 1993, the Hubble Space Telescope detected a binary star located in the heart of the constellation Sagittarius. One of the two stars was an extremely dense neutron star that was slowly devouring its white-dwarf star companion.

Sometimes a neutron star spins as it is being formed, sending out narrow beams of light. We only see this light when the spinning star aims its beam in our direction. The star looks like it is blinking on and off, or pulsing, much like a lighthouse. This kind of neutron star is called a pulsar. Pulsars were discovered in 1967 and identified as rapidly rotating neutron stars. If a neutron star continues to contract, it eventually becomes a black hole—a region around a dead star that is so dense that light cannot escape from it.

This artist's illustration of a pulsar shows a very bright star. Pulsars appear to blink on and off.

How the Universe Recycles

Stars never waste their material. Whenever a star dies, it leaves behind enough gas and dust for new stars to be created. This process has been going on for billions of years, since the universe began.

In the same way that dead plants decompose to form soil that supports the growth of new plants, the corpse of a star contains the material for a new generation of stars. Even the atoms in our own human bodies were once part of a star. Like the Sun and the planets of our solar system, we were born out of the same material that exists in the universe and in our atmosphere.

Everything is made of stardust—animals, plants, rocks, and metals. Nearly all the atoms in our bodies and in the earth were once part of a star that exploded and disintegrated. Those same atoms were the debris of an earlier star. Atoms never die; they just recycle themselves into new forms.

For millions of years, a dead star's gas and dust float and travel through outer space, waiting for gravity to start the process of building a new star. All the ingredients are there—the hydrogen and helium, and the dust particles. Recycling is not a new concept at all. It's been going on since the beginning of the universe.

arms The long appendages that reach out from the center of a spiral galaxy.

asterism An easily recognizable group of stars within a constellation.

astronomer A person who studies the science of the stars and planets.

atom The smallest particle of a chemical element that has the chemical properties of that element.

axis An imaginary line around which a body, such as a planet, rotates.

binary Something that is composed of two things or parts, as in a binary star.

black hole A region of the universe in which a very large mass is concentrated into a very small (essentially zero) volume. Scientists still disagree as to whether black holes actually exist.

Cepheids Yellow supergiant stars that pulsate over a period of hours or days. The longer the period, the brighter the star.

constellation A group of stars that creates a pattern.

corona The outermost part of a galaxy.

diameter The length across an object, measured through its center.

Doppler effect A shift in light or sound waves that signals whether an object is moving toward or away from an observer.

equator An imaginary circle that divides the surface of a planet, like Earth, into two parts—the Northern and Southern Hemispheres.

extraterrestrial Anything that exists outside of Earth and its atmosphere.

galactic cluster An open cluster located in a galaxy.

galactic year The period of time it takes the Sun to revolve around the Milky Way galaxy.

globule The early phase of a star's development when gas molecules and dust come together to form a ball.

gravity The force of attraction between two bodies.

halo In a galaxy, the region that extends above and below the disk.

hemisphere The northern or southern half of Earth, divided by the equator.

interstellar Located between or among the stars.

luminosity The amount of light that an object gives off; the state of being luminous.

Magellanic Clouds The two galaxies nearest to the Milky Way.

matter The substance of which an object is composed.

nebula An immense cloud of gas and dust in which stars may be born.

neutron star A very dense object left after a large star has exploded and given off most of its mass.

nova A star that suddenly becomes brighter and then gradually fades.

nuclear bulge A sphere of star matter in the center of a spiral galaxy.

nucleus The center of a star or galaxy.

open cluster A group formed in a nebula by developing stars.

optical telescope A telescope that uses light to make objects easier to see.

orbit The path that an object follows as it travels around another object.

planetary nebula A huge, shining circle of gas left by a dying star.

protoplanetary disks Flattened disks of dust and gas spinning around some stars.

protostar A ball of gas and dust that is an early version of a mature star.

pulsar A kind of neutron star that is bright and appears to blink on and off.

solar system This term usually refers to the system in the Milky Way that includes the Sun and its planets. Scientists have recently discovered that there are other solar systems in the universe.

stellar Something relating to the stars.

supernova An enormous explosion that occurs in space during which a star expels all or most of its mass.

theory An idea or belief that has not yet been proven.

universe All of the celestial objects together with the space in which they are found.

vacuum A space that contains no matter.

variable star A star whose brightness constantly changes.

FURTHER READING

Barbree, Jay and Martin Caidon. *A Journey Through Time: Exploring the Universe with the Hubble Space Telescope*. New York: Viking Studio Books, 1995.

Bonnet, Robert L. *Space and Astronomy: 49 Science Fair Projects*. Blue Ridge Summit, PA: TAB Books, 1992.

Branley, Franklyn M. *The Sun and the Solar System*. New York: Twenty-First Century Books, 1996.

Cosmic Mysteries. Alexandria, VA: Time-Life Books, 1990.

Croswell, Ken. *The Alchemy of the Heavens: Searching for Meaning in the Milky Way*. New York: Anchor/Doubleday, 1995.

Docekal, Eileen M. *Sky Detective: Investigating the Mysteries of Space*. New York: Sterling, 1992.

George, Michael. *Stars*. Mankato, MN: Creative Education, 1991.

Moore, Patrick. *The Stars*. Brookfield, CT: Copper Beech Books, 1995.

Procellino, Michael R. *A Young Astronomer's Guide to the Night Sky*. Blue Ridge Summit, PA: TAB Books, 1991.

Ridpath, Ian. *The Facts On File Atlas of Stars and Planets: A Beginner's Guide to the Universe*. New York: Facts On File, 1993.

ON-LINE

For current news and information for the amateur astronomer, visit *Astronomy* magazine's home page. It can be found at http://www.kalmbach.com/astro/astronomy.html

For information about all the latest discoveries and events in space, visit *Sky and Telescope* magazine's website at http://www.skypub.com/s_t/s_t.html

Visit the NASA home page for current information about NASA and its space programs. The site also links to other NASA agencies. It can be found at http://www.gsfc.nasa.gov/NASA_homepage.html

The Northern Colorado Astronomical Society website provides information and a monthly newsletter for amateur astronomers. It also provides links to other astronomy sites. It can be found at http://lamar.ColoState.EDU/~rmoench/ncasrdm.html

The North American Skies site has information about planets, eclipses, meteor showers, and other celestial events. Visit it at http://members.aol.com/astroclass/

SOURCES

Becklake, Sue. *Space: Stars, Planets, and Spacecraft.* New York: Dorling Kindersley, 1991.

Ferris, Timothy, editor. *The World Treasury of Physics, Astronomy and Mathematics.* Boston: Little Brown and Co., 1991.

Galaxies. Alexandria, VA: Time-Life Books, 1988.

Gibbons, Gail. *Stargazers.* New York: Holiday House, 1992.

Microsoft Encarta '96 Encyclopedia (CD-ROM). Redmond, WA: Microsoft Corporation, 1993–1995.

New York Public Library. *Science Desk Reference.* New York: Macmillan, 1995.

Ronan, Colin A. *The Universe Explained.* New York: Henry Holt, 1994.

Simon, Seymour. *Galaxies.* New York: Morrow Junior Books, 1988.

Space and Planets. Alexandria, VA: Time-Life Books, 1992.

INDEX